IGNATIUS

OF ANTIOCH

THE MAN WHO FACED LIONS

HEROES OF THE FAITH

THE BANNER OF TRUTH TRUST

3 Murrayfield Road, Edinburgh EH12 6EL, UK
P.O. Box 621, Carlisle, PA 17013, USA

*

© Sinclair B. Ferguson 2010

*

ISBN-13: 978 1 84871 093 1

*

Typeset in Times New Roman 15/18 at
The Banner of Truth Trust, Edinburgh

Printed in the U.S.A. by
Versa Press, Inc.,
East Peoria, IL

*

IGNATIUS

OF ANTIOCH

THE MAN WHO FACED LIONS

SINCLAIR B. FERGUSON

ILLUSTRATED BY ALISON BROWN

THE BANNER OF TRUTH TRUST

TABLE OF CONTENTS

THE GOOD NEWS SPREADS

IT is 2,000 years now since Jesus Christ came into our world. He was born in the little town of Bethlehem, far away from the great city of Rome. In those days the Roman Emperors ruled over the land of his birth.

The New Testament tells us how Jesus obeyed his heavenly Father perfectly.

During the last three years of his life Jesus did many wonderful miracles — healing the sick, giving sight to the blind, making the deaf to hear and the dumb to speak. On a few occasions he brought people back to life again shortly after they had died.

BUT Jesus came into the world to do much more than that. He was given the name 'Jesus', which means 'Saviour'. He came to save his people from their sin.

THE Bible teaches us that because of our sins we deserve to die.
Jesus came to die for our sins.
God accepted the sacrifice he made for us.
He raised Jesus, his Son, from the dead.

JESUS IS NOW ALIVE!

For almost six weeks after his resurrection, Jesus met with his little group of disciples to teach them what they were to do.

Then he went back to heaven.

BEFORE the Lord Jesus went back to heaven he told his disciples to go to every country in the world. He said:

'Tell the good news of the gospel to every man and woman, and to every boy and girl.'

The disciples listened very carefully to what he said.

How could they do this? There were so few of them.

But Jesus promised that he would send his Holy Spirit to help them.

ON the Day of Pentecost the Holy Spirit came to them. He gave them power to be witnesses to Jesus, first in Jerusalem, and then in Judea and Samaria, and then in every country.

The New Testament tells us what happened to some of the disciples afterwards.

SIMON Peter preached in many places. One day God sent him to preach in the home of a Roman centurion called Cornelius. Many people who were not Jews became Christians.

JAMES, the brother of John, died very bravely. King Herod cruelly put him to death.

But what about the others?

THOMAS (we usually call him 'Doubting Thomas', although he became 'Thomas the Believer') almost certainly went as far away as India to tell people there about Jesus.

The other disciples went to many different countries.

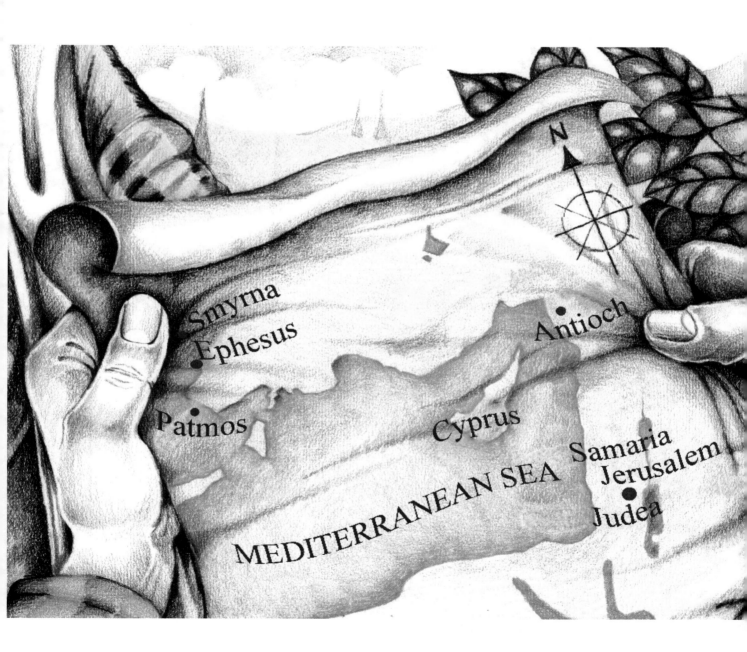

JOHN wrote the fourth Gospel. He also travelled to far away cities.

Later John was punished for being a believer in Jesus and was sent to the island of Patmos.

There John had an amazing vision, which he wrote down in the book of the Bible called Revelation.
He then sent it to churches in what we today call the country of Turkey.

JOHN lived to be an old man. His Christian friends loved him very much, and younger people really liked him too!

Two Friends

Two of these younger Christians became close friends. One of them was called Polycarp. His friend was named Ignatius. He was also sometimes called Theophorus, which means 'God-Carrier'.

Ignatius and Polycarp became ministers, or bishops. ('Bishop' comes from a Greek word that means 'over-seer.') In the New Testament a 'bishop' is also called an 'elder.' He is someone who helps to lead the church.

Bishops Ignatius and Polycarp lived in two different cities. They were also very different kinds of people! Ignatius means something like 'On Fire.' That was certainly a good name for him. Ignatius was a bishop in Antioch, the city where Jesus' followers were first called Christians.* Polycarp was a bishop in Smyrna, which was over six hundred miles away from Antioch.

---

* We learn this from Acts chapter 11 verse 26.

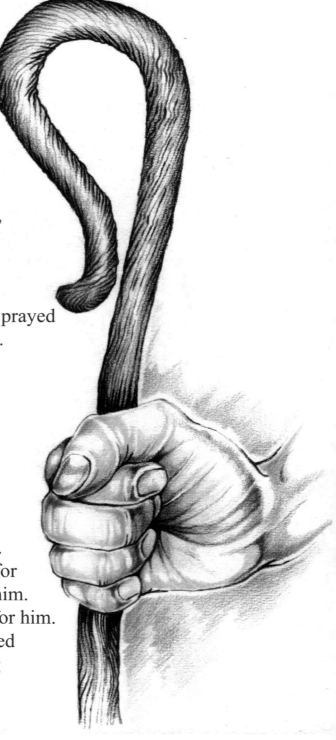

IN those days it was often dangerous to be a disciple of Jesus.

The Roman Emperor, Domitian, persecuted people who did not believe in the religion of the Roman Empire. He called them 'atheists' because they did not believe in the Roman 'gods'.

Since Christians believed in the Lord Jesus, and not in the false Roman 'gods', it must have been a very worrying time for them.

IGNATIUS loved his Christian friends. He prayed all the time that God would protect them. Bishops or ministers are commanded in Scripture to be shepherds of God's people. Ignatius cared for the Lord's flock. He would have been prepared to give his life for them.

But for the moment he did not need to.

Ignatius wanted to give everything to Jesus. After all, Jesus had spoken about the need for his disciples to take up the cross to follow him. He had also spoken about giving your life for him. So far Ignatius knew that Jesus had not asked him to sacrifice his life. But he was willing to do it.

THE EMPEROR TRAJAN

SOME time later there was a new Roman Emperor whose name was Trajan. We know what Trajan thought about Christians because he wrote a letter to one of his Governors, a man called Pliny. He told him what to do about followers of Jesus. Here is what the Emperor Trajan wrote:

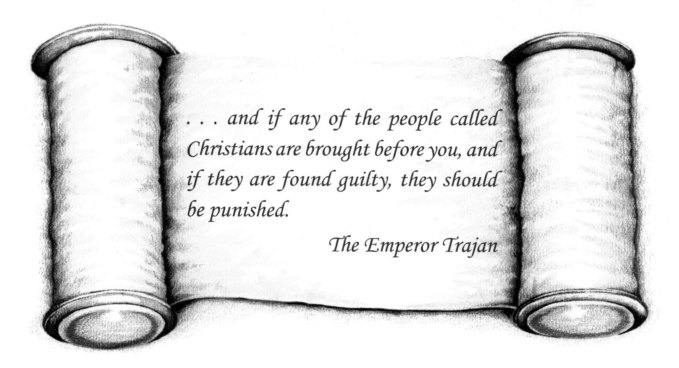

. . . and if any of the people called Christians are brought before you, and if they are found guilty, they should be punished.

The Emperor Trajan

Anyone who did not acknowledge the gods of Rome and make sacrifices to them was to be tried and put to death. Ignatius refused to worship these idols.

IGNATIUS wanted to protect his congregation. He loved them very much. He decided that if anyone was to be put on trial, it must be himself. Perhaps if he was punished his Christian friends would be left in peace.

ONE day Emperor Trajan came to Antioch. It was the third largest city in the Roman Empire. Ignatius, the man who would not bow to Roman gods, was brought to stand trial before him.

NOW was the time for Ignatius to be brave. His choice was very clear. Sacrifice to the Roman gods — or die!

The Emperor Trajan despised Ignatius. Who did this man think he was to stand against the Roman Empire? How dare he defy the most powerful man in the world?

'**Y**OU wicked, wretched man! You are defying the gods!' said the Emperor when Ignatius was brought to see him, bound in chains.

IGNATIUS replied: 'No one should call Theophorus (his other name) wicked. God has delivered me from all wickedness. And I do defy your gods, because they are just idols. They are false gods. They are not real at all!'

'**W**HO is Theophorus?' shouted Trajan, trying to frighten Ignatius.

'**I** am someone in whose life Jesus Christ the King of heaven dwells', Ignatius replied. Then he began to confess his faith in Jesus as Lord. He told the Emperor what all true Christians believed:

'**I** BELIEVE that there is only one God. He is the one who made heaven and earth, the sea and the sky. And I believe that there is only one Saviour. He is Jesus Christ, the Son of God. The kingdom of Christ is already here. It is the joy of Christians to belong to it!'

TRAJAN was really angry now. How dare this man say that Jesus is Lord!
He shouted back, 'Do you believe in that Jesus who was crucified under
Pontius Pilate? You wretched man!'

'Yes', replied Ignatius, 'he was crucified. But through him my sin and my
enemy the Devil have been crucified. Now he lives in our hearts!'

'Well then, Ignatius', said the Emperor, 'do you dare to tell me that you carry
with you the one who was put to death by being crucified? Then let Ignatius
taste what it means to be put to death!'

TRAJAN shouted at the soldiers,

'Take him out of my sight! Take
the prisoner to Rome. Let the
lions have him for their meat!
Let the citizens of Rome have his
death for their entertainment.
Get him out of my sight!'

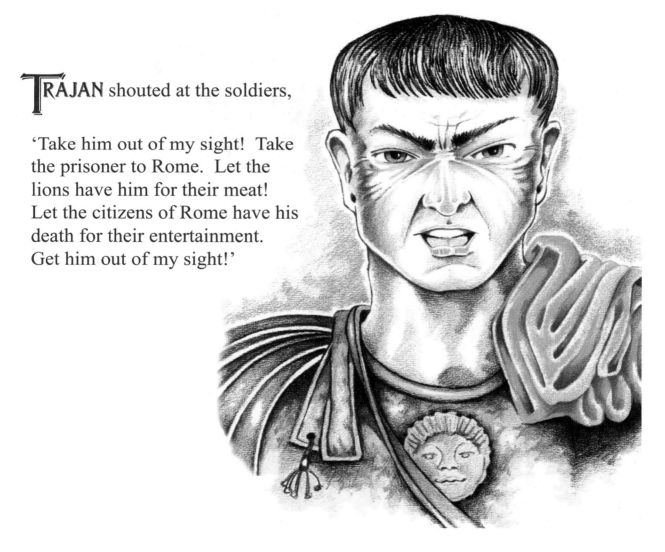

THEN something amazing happened. It completely surprised Trajan and his officers . . .

Although he was bound by chains Ignatius shouted out for joy!

Then, he prayed to the Lord Jesus,

'Lord Jesus, thank you for counting me worthy to suffer for you.'

And then he prayed again. But now there were tears in his eyes.

'Lord Jesus, please watch over your church, which I have tried to care for as its bishop. Please bless them and keep . . .'

But as he was praying the rough soldiers pulled him away.

As soon as they could they started on the long journey to Rome.

It was not going to be an easy journey for Ignatius.

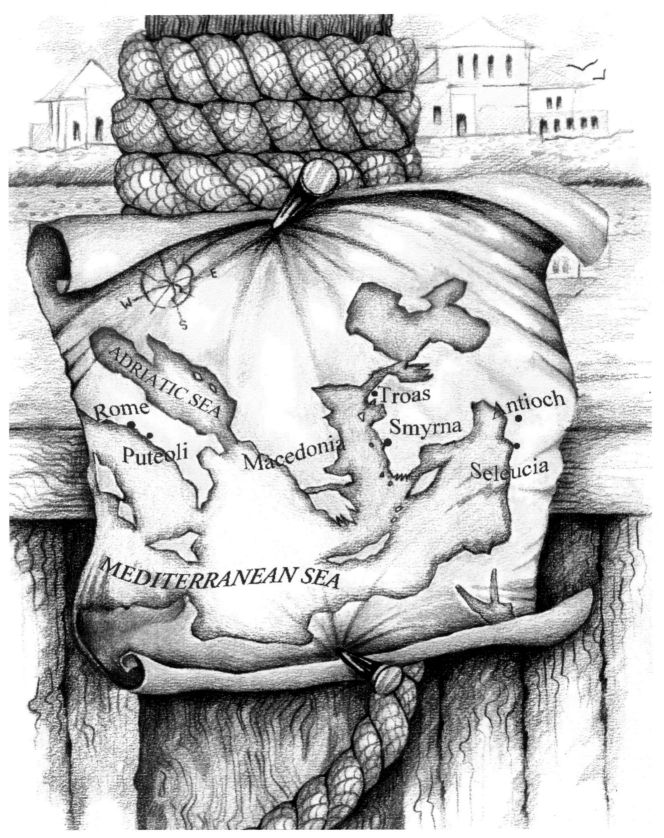

ON THE WAY TO ROME

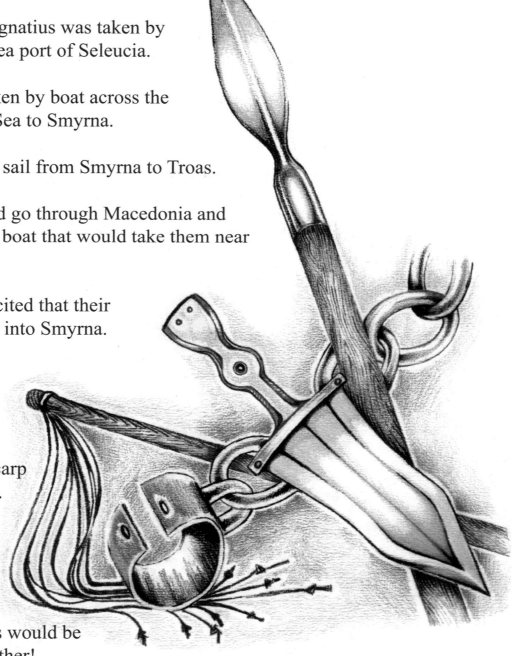

FIRST of all Ignatius was taken by road to the sea port of Seleucia.

Then he was taken by boat across the Mediterranean Sea to Smyrna.

The plan was to sail from Smyrna to Troas.

Then they would go through Macedonia and eventually get a boat that would take them near to Rome.

Ignatius was excited that their boat was sailing into Smyrna.

Can you guess why?

Yes, of course! His friend Polycarp lived in Smyrna.

He was the bishop of the church there.

The two bishops would be able to talk together!

VISITING SMYRNA

WHEN Ignatius got off the boat at Smyrna, his first question was, 'Can you take me to the home of Polycarp?' Ignatius always seemed to be in a hurry. So, as soon as he found out where Polycarp lived, he was in a hurry to get there.

WHAT a reunion they had! What stories they had to tell each other and what memories they shared.

How wonderful it was for them to be able to pray together.

IGNATIUS was able to meet all the Christians in Polycarp's congregation. He told them what had happened. He explained to them why he was so willing to go to Rome to face the lions.

OF course they wanted to try to save his life. But Ignatius said that they must not do that. He even wrote a letter from Smyrna to the Christians in Rome. He asked them not to do anything to try to protect him.

Here is part of what he wrote . . .

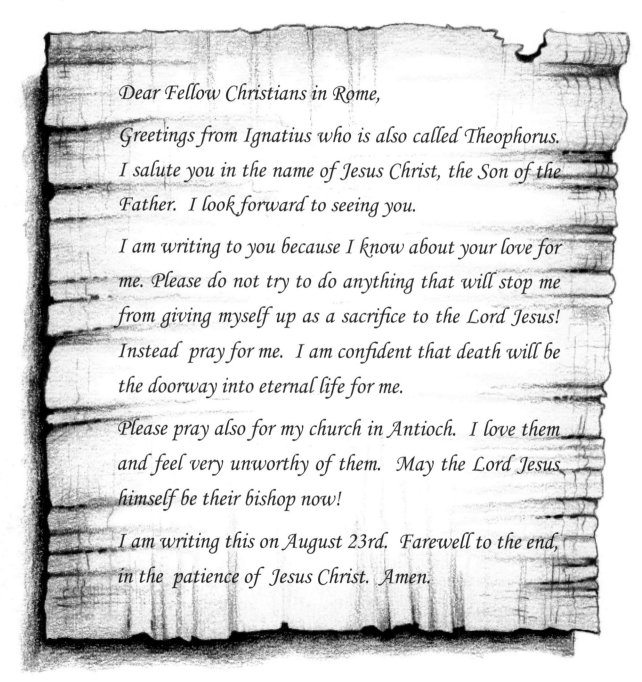

Dear Fellow Christians in Rome,

Greetings from Ignatius who is also called Theophorus. I salute you in the name of Jesus Christ, the Son of the Father. I look forward to seeing you.

I am writing to you because I know about your love for me. Please do not try to do anything that will stop me from giving myself up as a sacrifice to the Lord Jesus! Instead pray for me. I am confident that death will be the doorway into eternal life for me.

Please pray also for my church in Antioch. I love them and feel very unworthy of them. May the Lord Jesus himself be their bishop now!

I am writing this on August 23rd. Farewell to the end, in the patience of Jesus Christ. Amen.

SOMETHING wonderful happened while Ignatius was in Smyrna. Bishops from other churches and some other leaders came to meet with him. Best of all, of course, he was able to spend time with Polycarp. But soon the impatient soldiers took him down to the sea port. They wanted to get to Rome as quickly as possible.

IGNATIUS was very kind to these soldiers. There were ten of them. They took it in turns to guard him. But when Ignatius was kind to them, they were only cruel to him.

Perhaps they felt guilty about what they were doing. That sometimes makes people act in a horrid way to Christians.

But these men were so cruel that even Ignatius said it was like being chained to ten leopards!

Can you imagine how horrible that must have been?

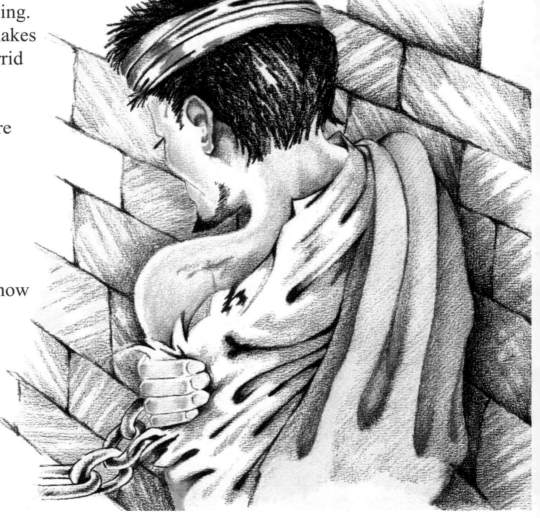

IGNATIUS WRITES SOME LETTERS

IGNATIUS was full of love. When his friends had all gone back home, he sat down to write letters to them.

He first wrote a letter to the church in Rome, the city to which he was travelling.

Then he wrote other letters, to the churches at Ephesus, Magnesia, and Tralles, as well as to the church in Philadelphia.

He also wrote a letter to the church in Smyrna that had come to love him and care for him so much.

These letters were kept, and down through the years they were copied, so that today we still know what Ignatius wrote.

WE also know what was on his heart as he went to Rome to be a witness for the Lord Jesus.

In his letters he kept mentioning three things . . .

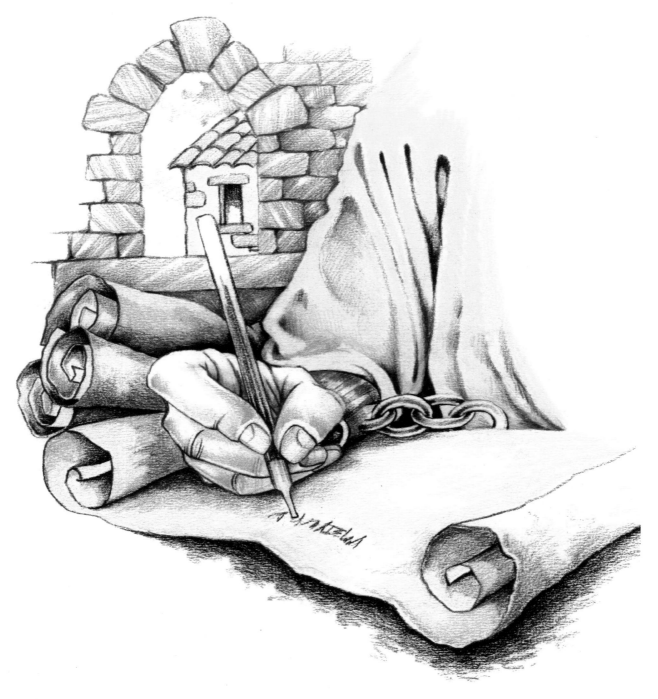

FIRSTLY, Ignatius remembered that Jesus had commanded his disciples to love each other. He had heard about that from the Apostle John, because John recorded the Lord's words in his Gospel: 'A new command I give to you, that you love one another: just as I have loved you, you also are to love one another.'*

Why is that important?

When Christians love each other they show that the love of the Lord Jesus has changed their lives. Then people who are not yet followers of Jesus will notice the change, and want to learn about Jesus for themselves.

---

* John chapter 13 verse 24.

SECONDLY, Ignatius warned the churches against false teachers who taught wrong things about Jesus.

Some people were teaching that if you were going to be a true Christian you needed to do Jewish things as well as trust in Jesus as your Saviour.

But John had taught Ignatius that Jesus had come to save Gentiles as well as Jews. You do not need to do Jewish things to follow Jesus! What you need to do is to trust in him and turn away from the old sinful way of life.

Other people were teaching that Jesus was not a real man.

But if Jesus were not a real man he could never be the Saviour of real men and women and real boys and girls, could he? If Jesus were not a real man he could not have died on the cross for our sins. But, said Ignatius, talking about the Lord Jesus, 'My Love is crucified.'

THIRDLY, Ignatius asked all of his new friends to pray for his church in Antioch. Ignatius was praying for the believers there, that the Lord Jesus would watch over them and use them for his glory.

When he got to Troas, Ignatius also wrote a letter to the Christians in Smyrna. He was so happy to see their love and their faith! He was very grateful for their care and concern for him. He told them to follow Polycarp's leadership and to honour him. No wonder! His friend Polycarp was an amazing Christian!

There was one more very special letter Ignatius wanted to write.

Can you guess to whom this one was sent?

It began . . .

Greetings!

Ignatius, who is also called Theophorus,
to Polycarp, Bishop of the Church of Smyrna
or rather, who has as his own Bishop,
God the Father and the Lord Jesus Christ.

May tremendous happiness be yours!

YES, Ignatius wrote a special letter just for Polycarp. He gave him all kinds of advice about being a good minister.

He knew he was not better than his friend Polycarp. So he reminded him of what the Apostle Paul had written to his young friend Timothy, when he had been the bishop of Ephesus.

Here are just some of the things Ignatius wrote to Polycarp . . .

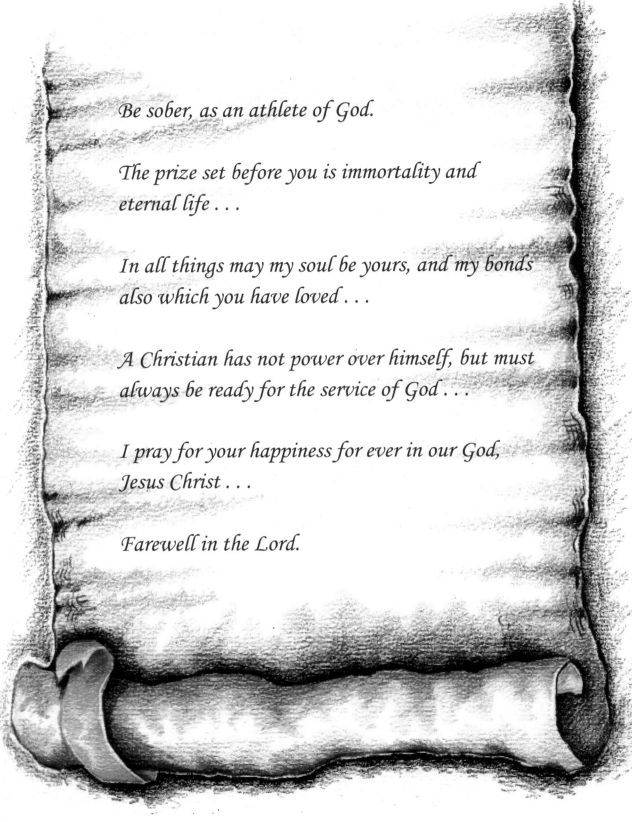

Be sober, as an athlete of God.

The prize set before you is immortality and eternal life . . .

In all things may my soul be yours, and my bonds also which you have loved . . .

A Christian has not power over himself, but must always be ready for the service of God . . .

I pray for your happiness for ever in our God, Jesus Christ . . .

Farewell in the Lord.

WHAT must Polycarp have felt when he read those last four words?
Did he ask himself, 'I wonder if the day will come when I, Polycarp, will need to remember these words of encouragement, and be strong and brave like my dear friend Ignatius?'

The Lions of Rome

THE soldiers took Ignatius and two other prisoners from Troas to Neapolis. They went by foot through Macedonia and then sailed across the Adriatic Sea. They wanted to disembark at Puteoli, but the winds were too strong for them to stop there. Instead they sailed on into Portus, the port of Rome.*

THE end came very quickly now for Ignatius. Some of the Christians in Rome met him when he arrived. He had to tell them not to try to save his life. 'Instead', he said, 'Let us pray together.'

The chains rattled noisily as Ignatius struggled to kneel down beside them. He prayed with them . . . 'Lord Jesus, we pray for the church you have been building throughout the world. It is your church, Lord. Be with your children!'

'Show your sovereign power and bring this wicked persecution to an end!'

'Fill your people with love for one another that the world may see your saving power in our lives.'

Ignatius had now reached the end of his journey.

---

* See the map on page 18.

TRAJAN wanted to have Ignatius thrown to the lions. That was part of the horrible entertainment that people enjoyed. But the games were already coming to an end for the day. The soldiers hurried Ignatius on into the city, and then to the Colosseum, the huge stadium in Rome.

WE cannot be certain in what year all this took place. But we know the exact day. It was what the Romans called 'Day 13 before the Kalends of January.' We call that day the 20th of December. It was at the time of the Roman holiday called Saturnalia. It was late in the afternoon, but there was still a large crowd of people at the games. The Colosseum held over fifty thousand people.

IGNATIUS was dragged into the centre of the arena. The soldiers left him there alone.

THE lions' cages were opened . . .

IGNATIUS knew the teaching of Jesus. He knew by heart the words of Jesus that the Apostle John had recorded in his Gospel.

'If the world hates you, know that it has hated me before it hated you . . . If they persecuted me, they will also persecute you.'*

He knew that Jesus had died for his sins, and he trusted him as his Saviour. But he also knew that Jesus had risen again from the grave.

Jesus had conquered the powers of darkness, sin, and death.

IGNATIUS was sure that even the horrible death he was going to die would be like a door opening into the presence of the Lord Jesus. Soon he would be near his Saviour in heaven. He would be with the Lord for ever!

He believed that false teaching should be feared more than martyrdom. The lions could kill only his body. But false teaching, whether it was the false teaching of the Roman Emperor, or the false teaching of people who pretended to be Christians, could kill his soul forever.

_____

* John chapter 15 verses 18-20.

LATE that afternoon, Ignatius of Antioch died for his faith in Jesus. He would not worship any false 'god' or sacrifice to an idol. He remained faithful to the Lord Jesus right to the very end. He knew that his death was just the beginning of everlasting life with Jesus.

The friends of Ignatius described him in these words:

IGNATIUS OF ANTIOCH
ALSO CALLED
THEOPHORUS

CHAMPION
AND
NOBLE MARTYR OF CHRIST

HE TROD UNDER FOOT THE DEVIL.
HE FINISHED THE COURSE WHICH,
FOR LOVE OF JESUS CHRIST,
HE DESIRED TO COMPLETE.

TO JESUS CHRIST,
TOGETHER WITH THE FATHER,
AND THE HOLY SPIRIT,
BE GLORY FOR EVERMORE.
AMEN!

GOD gives his servants great courage. He gives them greater confidence than they could ever have in themselves. He helps them to say things that are so bold that when we hear about them now we are simply amazed.

IN this way the Lord Jesus keeps his promise to his disciples that in their hour of need, but not before, he will give them the courage they lack and the words to speak.*

_____

* Jesus' words can be found in Luke chapter 12 verse 12.

IGNATIUS lived and died believing that Jesus would always be with him. Here is what he wrote beforehand to the Christians in Rome . . .

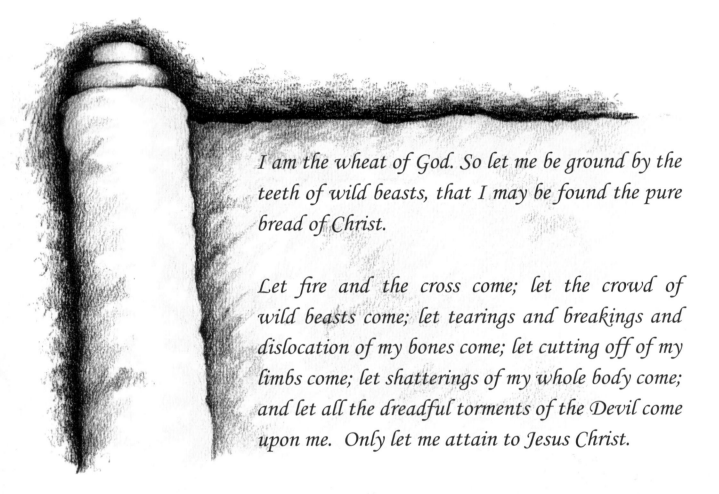

I am the wheat of God. So let me be ground by the teeth of wild beasts, that I may be found the pure bread of Christ.

Let fire and the cross come; let the crowd of wild beasts come; let tearings and breakings and dislocation of my bones come; let cutting off of my limbs come; let shatterings of my whole body come; and let all the dreadful torments of the Devil come upon me. Only let me attain to Jesus Christ.

WE do not face lions the way Ignatius did. But he also knew people he called 'leopards' who hated the Lord Jesus and were unkind to him. And so do we. We need courage to be Christians. We need the help of the Lord Jesus to know what to say when our faith is under attack.

Jesus has promised us this help. He said that he would be with his people to the ends of the earth and to the end of time.

THE story of *Ignatius — The Man who Faced Lions,* teaches us that Jesus keeps his promises, and that he is with his people always and everywhere.

ABOUT IGNATIUS OF ANTIOCH

Ignatius of Antioch – The Man who Faced Lions is a true story.

Ignatius was born when the Apostle John was still alive. We do not know the exact date.

His parents were possibly not Christians. But Ignatius became a follower of the Lord Jesus and then became minister of the church in Antioch.

Antioch was an important city in the Roman Province of Syria and had a population of about 100,000 people.

Ignatius was arrested and sent to Rome probably around the year 117 A.D.

On his journey, Ignatius did meet up with Polycarp in Smyrna. You can read about him in *Polycarp of Smyrna — The Man whose Faith Lasted*. Polycarp lived to be an old man. During his life he taught many people about the Lord Jesus. One of them became a great teacher too. You can read about him in *Irenaeus of Lyons — The Man who Wrote Books*.

We can still read copies of the letters Ignatius wrote to the churches who sent messengers to meet with him. These letters were collected by Polycarp after Ignatius died.

HEROES OF THE FAITH

HEROES OF THE FIRST CENTURIES	HEROES OF THE TRUTH	HEROES OF THE DARKNESS AND THE DAWN	HEROES OF THE REFORMATION

IGNATIUS ?-117
POLYCARP 70-156
  IRENAEUS 130/40-200

        ATHANASIUS 296-373
          BASIL OF CAESAREA 329-379
          GREGORY OF NYSSA 330-395
        GREGORY OF NAZIANZUS 330-389
            AUGUSTINE 354-430

              GOTTSCHALK 805-869
              ANSELM 1033-1109
                JOHN WYCLIFFE 1329-84
                  JAN HUSS 1373-1415

                        MARTIN LUTHER 1483-1546
                        WILLIAM TYNDALE 1494-1536
                          JOHN CALVIN 1509-64
                          JOHN KNOX 1514-72

BIRTH OF JESUS
B.C./A.D.
1/1---100--200-----300----400-------------1100------------1400--------------1500--------------

TIMELINE

HEROES OF THE
PURIFYING

HEROES OF
EVANGELISM

HEROES OF
THE WORLD

HEROES OF THE
20TH CENTURY

WILLIAM PERKINS 1558-1602
JOHN OWEN 1616-83
JOHN BUNYAN 1628-88

JOHN WESLEY 1703-92
JONATHAN EDWARDS 1703-1758
GEORGE WHITEFIELD 1714-1770

WILLIAM WILBERFORCE 1759-1833
WILLIAM CAREY 1761-1834
HENRY MARTYN 1781-1812
JOHN G. PATON 1824-1907

C. H. SPURGEON 1834-92
D. M. LLOYD-JONES 1899-1981

----------1600----------1700----------------------------1800----------1900------------2000

A Personal Word to Parents About Heroes of the Faith

Many of our children enjoy having heroes, but they are living in a world that encourages them instead to have 'idols'.

Sometimes, perhaps, the difference is simply a choice of words. But today it is usually more. For the 'idols' our children are encouraged to have — whether by media coverage or peer pressure — are to be 'adored' not because of their character, but because of their image.

By contrast a 'hero' is someone who is much more than a 'personality' about whom we may know little or nothing. A hero is someone who has shown moral fibre, who has overcome difficulties and opposition, who has been tested and has stood firm.

This series is about such people — heroes of the Christian faith — whose lives remind us of the words of Hebrews 13:7: 'Consider the outcome of their way of life, and imitate their faith.'

There are different kinds of heroes. The books in this series reflect the fact that some become heroes by being willing to die for Christ; others because of how they served the church of Christ; yet others because of what they taught about Christ; and others because of where they were prepared to go for Christ.

The HEROES OF THE FAITH books are intended to build up into a kind of church family album — pictures of those who, throughout the centuries, have been members of the family of God.

Many of us who are parents wish we could teach our children more about the story of the church, to help them see the privilege of belonging to a spiritual family that stretches back over the centuries and extends to the ends of the earth. This series aims to cover the centuries-long story of the church and to introduce children to heroes of the faith in every period of history.

None of these heroes was perfect — they all recognised their need of the Lord Jesus Christ as their Saviour and Lord. None of them claimed perfect understanding or perfect obedience. But each of them aimed to love the Lord with heart and mind and soul and strength. In that sense they were true heroes.

Many of these heroes were ministers and preachers of the gospel of Jesus Christ. But they were not heroes simply because they were ministers. The word 'minister' means 'servant'. They were people who became leaders in the church; they became heroes because they were servants both of the Lord Jesus and of his people.

I count it a privilege to have the opportunity of introducing your family, and especially your children, to these HEROES OF THE FAITH. May they become heroes too!

SINCLAIR B. FERGUSON